# For the Edification of the Saints

## By

## Dr. Lydia A. Woods

†††
**CWP**

*Channing and Watt Publishers*
*Atlanta, GA*

# Other Publications
## by Dr. Lydia A. Woods

*Acceptance with Joy*
*Poems by Revelation*
*Food for Saints*
*Let Those With Ears…*
*Conversations with the Saints*
*All the Saints Agree*
*Those Bible Characters*
*Lessons of a Handmaiden*
*The Movies: Their Spiritual Messages*
*The Joy of the Lord*
*Under the Rainbow*

Dedicated to
My Children
John, Geoffrey, Joseph, Elizabeth
And my Grandchildren
Deveraeux, John IV, Ayla, Jace,
Adia, Kheperu-t

# Acknowledgements

A piece of creative work is usually produced in isolation, but the distribution for others to see and appreciate takes many hearts and hands and minds. I want to give thanks to my friends and family members who are those hearts which support and lift me up and forward.

Special thanks to William C. Terry, Yehonatan Meru, and Veronica Norris for taking their time to proofread this book.

My appreciation to the host of colleagues, students and fellow Christian brothers and sisters who praise and encourage me and constantly remind me of the work God can do in a willing but frightened and fragile vessel.

Thank you Holy Spirit for using my humble vessel
and letting me put my name on these words.

# Introduction

Under the inspiration of the Holy Spirit, I began writing Christian Poetry. When I look back at the beginning, I realize now that I knew very little about the Holy Spirit and His relationship to me. At first, I would be awakened during the night, out of a sound sleep, with a poem forming in my head, or sometimes while driving, or in the midst of conversation with someone.

I would tell people that the Spirit would come and go, then months later return, to give me poems. My understanding has since grown, and I now know that the Spirit never leaves and is always present with me and in me and thru me – the two of us are one.

I believe the Holy Spirit, is God and that God exists in every human being. The real gift of life is discovering God within you, which first blesses you, then those around you.

These collections of poems are inspired by the lessons which the Lord has been teaching me as I walk with Him. Many poems are inspired by uplifting and stimulating conversations with God's precious Saints and others are born out of the frustration that many do not know the Love of God and His amazing grace and mercy.

In reading, I hope you will find poems which speak to your heart, express what you have experienced, or have enlightened your understanding. The writing of these poems allow me an outlet of spiritual expression, as the Lord tempers and prepares me for my Calling.

# Table of Contents

## Poems

Adult vs Child ................................................................ 1
But For Your Praying Saints ...................................... 3
Created in My Father's Image ................................... 5
Don't Envy Those ...................................................... 7
The Family Business .................................................. 9
Fear vs Faith ........................................................... 11
Go the Distance ...................................................... 13
God Will Provide ..................................................... 17
Group Three ............................................................ 19
Hedge of Protection ................................................ 21
How Many Times ..................................................... 23
How Will I Know Him? .............................................. 26
I Need the Eyes of Jesus ......................................... 27
If You Want to Make God Laugh! ............................. 29
In a Split Second ..................................................... 31
The Inside of the Cup .............................................. 35
It's Not About Money ............................................... 37
Oh! To be Like the Master ....................................... 39
Somethin' Told Me .................................................. 45
Take a Visit to the Upper Room .............................. 47
The Time is Short! ................................................... 51
Was He Saved? Did He Know the Lord? ................. 53

# Scriptural References

Adult vs Child .......................................................... 57
But For Your Praying Saints .................................. 58
Created in My Father's Image............................... 59
Don't Envy Those .................................................. 60
The Family Business ............................................. 61
Fear vs Faith......................................................... 62
Go the Distance .................................................... 63
God Will Provide ................................................... 69
Group Three ......................................................... 71
Hedge of Protection ............................................. 73
How Many Times .................................................. 75
How Will I Know Him? ........................................... 76
I Need the Eyes of Jesus...................................... 83
If You Want to Make God Laugh!........................... 84
In a Split Second................................................... 85
The Inside of the Cup ........................................... 86
It's Not About Money............................................. 87
Oh! To be Like the Master .................................... 89
Somethin' Told Me................................................. 90
Take a Visit to the Upper Room............................. 91
The Time is Short! ................................................ 93
Was He Saved? Did He Know the Lord?................ 96

**Scriptural Index**................................................. **98**

# Poems

# *Adult vs Child*

*Matthew 18:3; Proverbs 22:6; Luke 18:16 (KJV)*

As an adult, how many times have you thought?
In the good old days, I really had it made,
Mom and dad paid all of the bills,
I had it good, I had it made in the shade.

Now adulthood, is a relative term.
The world teaches you well indeed.
Everyone trying to get grown so fast,
Being responsible and planning to succeed.

That's what it takes in this world today,
A mature and responsible adult,
You'll have all of your dreams fulfilled,
But is that really the final result?

Why is it that the Father teaches,
Just the opposite of what the world sells,
To become as a little child....
Trusting in Him so you won't go to hell!

Now the author of kill, steal, and destroy,
Hates all of God's children; it's true,
He's mad as hell cause he can't inherit,
And I think he's just a little jealous, don't you?

So this adulthood is for the birds,
Go on, try being a child; there's no catch,
The Father wants all your troubles and cares,
Adult vs child - No Competition, not even a Match!

Dr. Lydia A. Woods

# But For Your Praying Saints

*Ephesians 6:18; I Thessalonians 5:17; James 5:16 (KJV)*

Look out Satan cause you've been uncovered,
The truth has been told by my spiritual brother,
Frank Peretti is the Saint that's blessed me well.
He reveals what's going on in the pit of hell.

When he reads his book, "*This Present Darkness*" on cassette,
I'm telling you Saints you will never regret.
Listening to this book will spiritually educate you,
It will give you insight on just what to do.

His book is all about Satan's demons as they plot and plan,
To destroy God's Saints and steal the souls of man.
But don't despair the Lord's warriors are in place.
He dispatches angelic forces and they're on the case.

Their weapons are mighty for strongholds come down,
And they are powered by Saints that aren't playing around.
He speaks of Saints who know just what to do,
Using the power of prayer as they were commanded to.

-3-

As those mighty prayers ascend to the throne.
They empower the angels and they make right the wrong.
They can take out Satanic demons left and right,
They make quick work of them in this spiritual fight.

My daughter and I play the tape over and over again,
We love to hear the ending, when the angels win,
And then there's our favorite line in all of the book,
As the demon breathes his last and takes one long look,

At the captain of the host his angelic enemy,
Now here's the part that thrills my daughter and me.
Before he is vanquished – he speaks deep and faint,
But for your praying saints.........

# Created in My Father's Image

**Philippians 2:6; Galatians 4:6 (KJV)**

If you see me you've seen my Father,
Though you and He may have never met.
I am the child of His seed,
I believe that He has no regrets,

For He knows that one day I will be,
A perfect reflection of Himself in me,

In so many ways I'm becoming like,
My Father that you do not see,
The way I think, behave, and speak,
It's amazing what He's doing in me.

He's laboring in love with me,
As the years of my growth go by,
Why He has cared, I may never know,
It may come clear before I die,

Or maybe sometime before then,
When my heart has been given away,
To the child of my very own seed,
I'll understand my Father's love that day.

It is the "Circle of Life," that just goes round,
For generations a marvelous plan,
The Lord wanted to share His greatest joy,
The Gift of Creation -- with His precious man.

Where would I be without my Father today?
This life He's made possible to me.
With love and security I have grown,
To be this person that you see.

I honor you Abba Father, not just today, but all my days,
Giving honor where honor is due.
Your child so humbly wants to express,
That her heart is full of love just for you!

# *Don't Envy Those*

*Malachi 3:13-18 (KJV)*

Do not envy those that seem, to prosper in their way,
I quote this scripture to myself every day,

They all seem to be prospering, and I'm left behind,
Serving the Lord, and sorting everything out in my mind,

I understand with my head, that soon the wicked will be cut down,
And in that final day, the Lord will not be found,

I know that He's preparing, his people to stand in the evil day,
We're being tempered in the fire, that's the Lord's unique way.

But there are days when my mind, and emotions get in the way,
As they buy their material things, take trips, and then to me say,

"Oh, Lydia where are you going, for vacation this year",
Or "Why don't you just buy a house, don't rent.... you're losing
money dear".

"Go on take out a loan, buy what your heart most desires,
Everybody is doing it, you know, it's what the world requires."

I sometimes get frustrated, and feel sorry for myself,
And then the Lord will show me, how blessed I am, by His wealth.

That He's blessed me so well, that I never should complain,
Then I want someone to kick me in the behind, because I feel so ashamed.

That I ever doubted His word, or murmured and complained,
I can't stand this flaw in myself, Lord please help me to change.

I can't change myself, even though I try every day,
I didn't make myself, I came into the world this way,

But I can cry out daily to the Father, to keep working on me,
For only He can make me like, his Son and from sin be free!

Dr. Lydia A. Woods

# *The Family Business*

*I Corinthians 3:7-9 (KJV)*

So you've been called into the family,
Congratulations you're on your way,
Let me give you just a glimpse,
Of the Family Business as it stands today!

The Father has cattle on thousands of hills,
His fields are green and vast to view,
His wealth and family are beyond compare,
The Harvest is plentiful, but the workers are few.

I bet you didn't know of the family business,
Our business in growing and harvesting Souls,
The harvesting is constant and ongoing,
We harvest Souls from the young to the old.

Only the Father knows when they have ripened,
He's been in the business since the beginning of time,
Can you imagine the size of His wealth,
Just contemplating it blows your mind.

You see my brothers and sisters are all overworked,
Planting seeds and watering the fields,
The Father has mandated the tares grow with the wheat,
But it's the Father that determines the yields,

The Father wants every family member,
To be committed to the family goals,
Not going in their own direction,
But getting in the fields and harvesting those Souls.

-9-

So if you haven't made that commitment,
Get with the Father for His plan for your life,
You'll find out that the pay and standard of living,
Can support a large family and even a wife!

The benefits far surpass any outside employment,
The health plan and insurance are absolutely free,
He has provided for all of your needs,
Talk to your many brothers and sisters and see!

Now in the beginning you start with the small jobs,
Your responsibilities increasing as you prove your worth,
But no matter the size of your job,
We all get paid the same, because of our birth.

I'm very proud of the family business,
Looking forward to new family members, to bring in that crop,
It gets hot in those fields and the work is tedious,
But quite rewarding and none of us, would ever think to stop.

Lift your head up with pride and don't tire,
Teach your children when they are young,
That the family business is where the future lies,
It's rewarding, never boring, and really quite fun!

# *Fear vs Faith*

*I John 4:18; Romans 8:15; Luke 12:32; Psalm 118:6 (KJV)*

My beloved, the world teaches fear!
Your inheritance from time of old.
In the garden it entered in,
To this day fear wants to claim your soul.

When fear has its perfect work,
Sin is produced and the harvest is ripe.
And when sin is finally complete,
Then death comes and claims your spiritual life.

But the Father did not give that Spirit of fear,
You know who is the author of that!
Remember it's a spirit that comes and goes,
But you can rebuke it and that's a fact!

The Father gives us a measure of faith,
So work it and build it up very strong,
Like those outward bodies you work on so much,
Build that faith and you will never go wrong!

Fighting fear is a daily steady routine,
'Cause the world taught you to fear so well,
But you can overcome this enemy,
That's trying to take your soul to hell.

Go on, walk in the faith that He's given,
You'll have plenty of trials to practice on,
Use that shield of faith, please the Father,
Watch fear take a hike and be gone!

Practice laughing in the face of fear,
Go on try faith, there's no catch.
You'll get better at it every day,
Fear vs Faith - No Competition, not even a Match!

# Go the Distance

*Revelation 2:1-29, 3:1-22 (KJV)*

I like a good mystery,
I've read many in my time,
I work out the details
And plots in my mind.

Can't wait for the ending,
For the author to tell,
Just who is the bad guy
And who's going to jail!

Well the Bible is the best mystery,
That I ever read,
It keeps me on edge,
So many plots in my head.

But I wouldn't get caught,
Not reading the end,
Cause to a mystery hound like me,
That's really an unforgivable sin.

So it really amazes me,
How so many can resist,
Reading the last chapter,
And all that good ending miss.

Even the name of that chapter,
Rings quite true,
"Revelation" reveals the whole book,
To me and to you.

The author was clever,
For not all can see,
The final outcome,
Of this amazing mystery!

So I'll reveal a little truth,
That few know,
Just what the overcomer receives,
When the distance they go.

For the race is not given,
To the swift or the strong,
But he that endures to the end,
Will never go wrong.

Now I found that the overcomer,
Will eat of the tree of life,
That tree in the garden,
Denied to Adam and his wife.

The overcomer will eat hidden manna,
Receive a stone of pure white,
A new name in that stone,
So John, the author, writes.

The overcomer gets power,
To rule over the nations,
Given by the Morning Star,
For the overcomer has learned His patience.

White raiment is given ,
To show that we are pure,
Our name in the Book of Life,
Of that you can be sure.

Before the Father,
Our Savior confesses our name,
Also to the Angels in Heaven,
Our triumph proclaim.

A Pillar in the Temple of God,
We'll stand tall and straight,
Bearing the Name of our God,
And His city, I can hardly wait.

Our Lord's new name will be written,
On us for all to see,
Sealed there forever,
Unto all eternity.

So go the distance,
And never faint or fear,
For your Salvation is at hand,
And Redemption is near.

Last, but not least,
The Lord has granted to thee,
To sit with Him in His throne,
Forever Saved and Free!

**-15-**

Dr. Lydia A. Woods

# God Will Provide

**Genesis 22:1-19  (KJV)**

For in Isaac shall thy seed be called,
And this Seed the one to save us all.

But it came to pass, God called to Abraham,
Behold, "Here I am, Lord what is your command.?

Sacrifice Isaac thy only son to Me,
Take him to a place I will show to thee.

Lay him on an altar a burnt offering make,
Abraham rose, only his son and provision did take.

Isaac inquired of his father and this is why,
Abraham said to Isaac – "my son, here am I."

Isaac said, "Behold, there is fire and wood,
But we need a lamb to make this offering good."

For the burnt offering where is the lamb,
Tell me this – my father Abraham?

-17-

God will provide himself a lamb, Abraham said,
Then he bound his only son to that altar bed.

He took the knife stretched forth his hand,
To slay his son – that was God's command.

Then the angel of the Lord called unto him,
Abraham, Abraham stay your hand my friend.

Here am I, your servant, what is thy Will?
The Angel said, I know now that you love God still.

Abraham turned – a ram was caught by his horns,
He called the place Jehovah Jireh on that morn.

Because he did not withhold the thing he loved,
Many blessings flowed from God above.

And in thy seed shall all nations be blessed,
God will Provide! – Every saint can attest!

# *Group Three*

*Matthew 8:12, 13:37-43; Luke 13:24-30 (KJV)*

I'm very, very concerned about those in group three,
Because this group feels they are saved and free,
I was a member of that group for many years,
That group lives in deception and has many fears.

The deception of this group is enormous indeed,
They profess to living by God's Holy creed,
They profess to knowing the Father and Son,
They profess to Salvation but they have none,

They go to church, some since their birth,
They think they'll go to heaven when they leave this earth,
They have never experienced a Spiritual moment with Christ,
There really is no relationship, but only sin in their life.

They are in denial about their relationship with God.
They front, 'cause they don't want others to think them odd,
It's the going thing, you know, in this day and age,
Dressing up, and attending church is all the rage.

They go to the big church on the corner, for all to see,
Or the medium or small church, it's a religious decree,
They have their activities and programs galore,
And the building programs that will give them more.

More rooms and space so that activities can grow,
It's a sad religious existence, I want you to know.
Because they are only fooling themselves,
As they pursue their illusions and gather their wealth,

For in that final day as they stand at the door,
The Lord will open and they will implore,
Entrance to His Holy place,
But He will not know their names or recognize their face.

He will say I never, ever knew you,
Because you didn't do, what I asked you to.
You had many plans and ways of your own,
But I was not a part of them, look at the seeds you've sown.

Now who are those that are in group two?
It's filled with sinners, not saved, what about you?
They know they live in sin and are lost as can be,
But group one is the light of the world, to help them see,

And of course group one are the children of God,
A peculiar people indeed – and kind of odd,
Living as examples of Christ, for all to know,
That God is real and loves them so.

So in group three, you're just a wanna-be,
Pretending to know the Lord, bound and not free.
Stumbling around, puffed up in self-righteousness and fear,
Recognize your sins today,
Group one will be praying for you all my dears!

Dr. Lydia A. Woods

# Hedge of Protection

*Psalm 91:1-16; I Peter 3:4-6 (KJV)*

You have placed your hedge of protection,
Around me tight as a drum,
No one can penetrate through it,
No, not anyone....

Within your hedge of protection,
Our relationship grows strong every day,
You're preparing me for my future,
This vessel you'll use in your special way.

I feel safe and warm in your hedge,
I can look out on the world and see,
All the men and women and their relationships,
They're in trouble and that once was me.

I once operated outside the Father,
In relationships made on my own,
Wreaking havoc in the lives of others,
Now I'm reaping what I have sown.

There's no fleshly feelings or burning,
For your hedge provides perfect peace,
And in my celibacy, I sometimes wonder,
When your hedge of protection will cease.

Lord I pray that Your hedge of protection,
Stays round me until the season comes,
For me to join with the mate You've selected,
And You and he and I become one.

**-21-**

# How Many Times

**Philippians 4:19 (KJV)**

How many times must I,
Snatch you from the jaws of the devourer,
For you to remember,
That I am there for you hour after hour.

How many times must I,
Meet your need,
For you to remember,
That you are my lamb that I will feed.

How many times must I,
Surprise you with the secrets of your heart,
For you to remember,
That it is sweet gifts to you that I wish to impart.

How many times must I,
Comfort you,
For you to remember,
That I will always be there to rescue.

How many times must I,
Bless your children,
For you to remember,
That I will carry your every burden.

**-23-**

How many times must I,
Put food on your table,
For you to remember,
That I will never forsake - I am more than able.

How many times must I,
Pay your bills,
For you to remember,
That to provide for you is my divine will.

How many times must I,
Keep you and your children in health,
For you to remember,
That My Son took your sickness onto Himself.

How many times before you will believe,
That I love you,
I will pursue you until you know,
That it is true.

Look back and count,
All that I have done,
I have blessed you so many times,
You can't remember every one.

**-24-**

When revelation knowledge comes to you,
Of my endless love,
Then you can move from this grievous place,
And I'll lift you far above,

The day to day pressures of this world,
Filled with fear and strife,
And greater things I can accomplish,
Through your precious life.

So remember when the enemy speaks to you,
Do what my Son taught you to,

Say, "It is written Satan, you have no power here".
Speak the Word with boldness and never fear,
That I will not honor my own Word when I hear.

How many times - they are endless, My Dear.

# How Will I Know Him?

*Genesis 24:1-67 (KJV)*

Many young girls ask their mothers,
Just how will I know I'm in love?
After many failed relationships and wounded heart,
I asked this question, of my Father above.

He said, "Not as the world giveth,
Select I a mate just for you,
A mate that's prepared and rooted in me,
Washed in my Blood, a creature brand new."

"How will I know him?" I asked the Father,
His reply was simple indeed,
"By his spirit, my dear, you can tell,
If he's in Me and born of My Seed.

His outer appearance won't move you,
This is not a matter of flesh,
The gentleness and love in his heart,
You'll want to forever caress.

The joining of our spirits,
Yours and his and Mine,
A perfect union made by My hand,
To be bound in the Spirit for all time.

His spirit will witness to you,
The heart of the man I will reveal,
You'll love his love of the Father,
And in our love your union, I'll seal."

**-26-**

# I Need the Eyes of Jesus

*Luke 4:18; Psalm 119:105; I Corinthians 3:16  (KJV)*

Oh how I long to see – me, with Jesus' precious eyes
For so long I have been blind, using Satan for my guide,

Satan tells me to step down; when it's up that I should go.
He tells me I am unattractive,
When I am clothed with light and glow,

He says that I am helpless, when power is in my hand,
He tells me I am crippled, when I only need to stand.

He says I will not make it,
When Jesus has already overcome,
He says, I've lost the fight, when I've only just begun.

He says that I will never,
Become the perfection in Jesus Christ,
He says that I'm a loser, and that he will take my life.

The blinders cover my eyes, so that truth will hide from sight,
They need only be removed
To make my vision quite alright.

Satan seeks not only, to kill, steal and destroy,
But blinding God's children, is the basis of his ploy.

I can hardly bear the light,
For my eyes are darkened inside this shell,
But without the vision you possess,
I will be defeated and end in hell.

I do not want to stumble and fall,
So give me vision for my task,
You said, I only had to knock,
Or only need to ask.

I'm asking you today,
To unlock the blindness, set me free,
Jesus make these blind eyes open,
I know you are the only key.

Your vast and wonderful greatness,
Inside my vessel I want to see,
I need the eyes of Jesus,
For my true self to be revealed to me.

# *If You Want to Make God Laugh!*

*Proverbs 19:21; Matthew 5:36; Isaiah 46:9-11  (KJV)*

The old folk used to say, "It's all in God's Hands,"
And if you want to make God laugh,
Just tell Him your plans!

That you're gonna do this and that,
You're over twenty-one and that's a fact,
You're big and bad, so much in control,
Do what you want 'cause you're grown and bold.

The world taught you well about the planning part,
Everybody does it, and that's being smart.
To become a responsible adult and grown,
You must get on the go, get a plan of your own.

The sooner you realize that you have no power,
To make things happen from hour to hour,
That you can't change one hair on your head,
That you didn't wake yourself up today to get out of bed.

That you're a little child who can't come in or go out,
It doesn't do any good to get mad or even pout.
Things are out of your control so get with the plan,
That everything is purposed by God's own hand.

**-29-**

You were bought with a price
Do you know just what that means,
You got to give it up,
No use making a childish scene.

Scripture says, "Many are the plans of a man,
But God's purposes will prevail throughout the land,"
Stop drowning in the sea of denial,
'Cause you're bound to Him all the while.

So if you want to make God laugh today,
Just open your mouth, let Him hear you say,
That you've got plans and you're gonna do this and that,
Watch the Hand of God just slap you Back!

**-30-**

# In a Split Second

*James 1:8; II Corinthians 10:5 (KJV)*

In a split second your mind,
Can conjure up disaster,
And your demise comes from,
The great deceiving master.

When trouble comes,
Your mind is as active as can be,
Ripe for the picking,
And panic sets in so thoroughly.

You have a vivid imagination,
That can lead you to the grave,
You worry and stress yourself out,
And then begin to behave,

Like a stressed out nut,
Running here and running there,
Your weight goes up or down,
Then you begin to lose your hair.

You live and feed on fear,
And that's your daily bread,
It's amazing all the scenarios,
That you are playing out in your head.

If you look back and count,
What never came to be,
You will realize that the Word of God,
Can set you free.

Free from worry and stress,
And every evil work,
Free from your own thoughts,
That can drive you berserk.

Cast down those vain imaginings,
That come into your head,
Satan puts them there because,
He wants to see you dead.

So stop this foolish worrying,
It will only shorten your life span,
Commit your future to the Lord,
Place yourself within His hand.

"Don't worry, be happy,"
As the songwriter* wrote one day,
Tell Satan to take a hike,
And pack his bags, be on his way.

And in that split second,
When panic takes you to your doom,
Change your perspective, keep the faith,
For faith rids you of the gloom.

After you cast down those vain imaginings,
This is what you do,
Apply the Word of God, to your situation,
As you were commanded to.

Believe what the Word says,
It's not based on how good you are,
But on God's Grace and Mercy,
And His Righteousness...By Far!


* "Don't Worry, Be Happy." by Bobby McFerrin

# The Inside of the Cup

**Matthew 23:25; Luke 11:39 (KJV)**

Hypocrites, vipers, in your fine array,
Dressed to the hilt strutting your stuff today.

All in your finery going to worship your God,
Sitting on those pews, to me you look quite odd.

For are we reading, the same Bible, you and me,
For I have looked and looked, but I just don't see.

I do read that the traditions of man choke the Word,
And in man's traditions the Word just cannot be heard.

The Word warns us not to take heed to the cup's outside,
But tend to the cleanliness inside where the spirit abides.

It is the world that has taught you to look your best,
But by outward appearance, you can never pass the Lord's test.

Look deeper my precious Saints, inside the inner man,
And you will find spirits that are weak, emaciated and bland.

Spirits that are starving, needing to be spiritually fed,
Even though the outward body looks healthy, not even near dead.

But it is near death, that they are in reality, you see,
God's reality is far above you and me.

But we can access the mind, of the living Christ,
By the gift of love that He gave, when He paid the price.

Take your cup for a cleansing, on the inside every day,
Now it's only His blood, that can clean it in such a way,

That can get out all stains, dirt, grease and grime,
Don't be deceived precious saints. No, Not this Time!

Dr. Lydia A. Woods

# *It's Not About Money*

*Luke 12:22-34; Matthew 6:25-34  (KJV)*

Oh! I'm finally really getting it,
I'm kind of a slow learner you see,
It's not about having a lot of money,
But putting my trust in thee,

It rains on the just and unjust,
Equally rain falls into every life,
But it's how you deal with the problems,
How you handle the grief and the strife.

Now everyone is feeling the pressure,
Life is stressful and everyone is running scared.
But do you have a place to run to,
When everyone else is losing their head?

I'm learning not to lose my cool,
When things seem to be going all astray,
It happens so often that I'm beginning to wonder,
Maybe this is just the norm for life today.

The Lord wants me to rely on Him,
Not on money to solve every ill,
It's not money I really need,
Because trust in the Lord is a better deal.

It's finally sinking into my thick skull,
The years of trial and tribulation is creating in me,
The ability to be lifted to a higher level,
Of Trust and Rest and Peace in thee....

# Oh! To be Like the Master

*John 8:12, 28-29, 31 (KJV)*

Oh! How I long to be like the Master,
Just think of how He carried Himself,
With a confidence and an assurance,
Of who He was, and of His Father's wealth.

It was this calm and peaceful demeanor,
The air of royalty and perfect peace,
That drew multitudes to listen so intently,
To Words that they hoped would never cease.

Now the Master was cool,
He had His act together,
For He knew who He was,
And what the Father would do.

He never doubted,
But spoke words filled with faith,
The Words of His Father,
As He has commanded - Us to.

At the wedding feast,
They all got anxious,
His mother, Mary asked Him to help out,
She was His mom, and didn't have a doubt.

He didn't break a sweat,
As he commanded them to fill,
All those jugs with water,
How they marveled at the Master's skill.

**-39-**

Now the sisters, Mary and Martha,
Were extremely upset,
Brother Lazarus had died,
And they had only, one regret,

That if the Master had been there,
He would not have died,
And they were in His face,
Wanting to know just why?

Why, had it taken Him so long,
To come to their heed,
For Lazarus was already decaying,
In the tomb, now there was no need.

The Master prayed to the Father,
For everyone to behold,
"Lazarus come forth" He spoke,
The Word strong and bold.

Now the Master was cool,
He had His act together,
He knew who He was,
And what the Father would do.

He never doubted,
But spoke words filled with faith,
The Words of His Father,
As He has commanded - Us to.

**-40-**

Those disciples worried,
And fear took them in that boat,
While the Master slept,
Things would be calm if He were woke.

So in panic they awaken Him,
To come to their aid,
He calmed the rain and the wind,
And then to them did bade.

Why did you trouble me?
Where was your faith?
How long must I suffer,
To teach you to live by God's good grace?

Know who you are in the Father,
And what He will do,
Be skillful in the Word,
That I am teaching you.

The people were all worried,
About the woman who had sinned.
Took her to the Master,
For Him to condemn.

But He just calmly asked, of their own sin,
And wrote in the sand,
They all dropped their stones,
And walked away – every man.

**-41-**

Now the Master was cool,
He had His act together,
For He knew who He was,
And what the Father would do.

He never doubted,
But spoke words filled with faith,
The Words of His Father,
As He has commanded – Us to.

The man came to the Master,
Cause his daughter was dying,
When the Master showed up,
they were weeping and crying.

For the daughter had died,
and they laughed at Him,
When He said she only slept,
They thought Him quite dim.

He commanded,
That everyone leave,
Into the house with faith,
In His Father He believed,

Then He commanded,
That she rise and be fed,
He blew their minds,
And this played with their heads

Now the Master was cool,
He had His act together,
He knew who He was,
And what the Father would do.

He never doubted,
But spoke words filled with faith,
The Words of His Father,
As He has commanded - Us to.

Oh! How I long to be like the Master,
It's badly needed today,
I want to emulate His confidence
And faith in such a way,

That I live up to the work He started,
Here on earth is the Master's trust,
And through His precious Holy Spirit,
That He has graciously placed - In us.

Oh! To be like the Master, we just Must!

# Somethin' Told Me

John 12:26; Ephesians 4:30; Luke 2:26 (KJV)

Somethin' told me,
I should have turned left when I turned right,
Somethin' told me,
I should have called her late last night,

Somethin' told me,
Not to say those unkind words,
Somethin' told me,
That my bill was due on the third,

Somethin' told me,
That you were not doing so well,
Somethin' told me,
That I could get that dress at the mall on sale,

Somethin' told me,
Not to pick up that phone or go into that room,
Somethin' told me,
That he wasn't the right bridegroom.

If I had a dollar,
For all the times I've heard,
But did not heed the gentle voice,
Or the light, urging, words,

**-45-**

Of the faint and fleeting sound,
Within my being,
Somethin' told me,
Without my knowing or my seeing.

The Somethin' told me,
One day not long ago,
Will you stop saying,
"Somethin'" told you so and so.

My name is not "Somethin',"
Please call my name out right,
My name is Holy Spirit,
And I live within you out of sight.

I was sent by my Master,
To lead and guide you into truth,
My job is to protect you,
Bring you to remembrance. Do you need proof?

Just open up my Word,
And read about Me for yourself,
My name is not "Somethin',"
But I'm your Lord – It's Me Myself!

Dr. Lydia A. Woods

# *Take a Visit to the Upper Room*

*Acts 1:3-4, 8, 2:1-21 (KJV)*

Have you ever visited the upper room?
Don't want to get in your business or assume,
That everyone knows just where it's at,
So let me lay it out in white and black.

Jesus told those disciples to go to that place,
Don't go anywhere else, to the room make haste.
For you can't witness or testify effectively,
Until the Holy Ghost comes, and gets in thee.

For you need special Power from on High,
To be successful in the fight and this is why,
Jesus got the Holy Ghost too, before the wilderness,
He battled with Satan, and He did effectively resist.

So how do you think you can do battle too,
If the Holy Spirit doesn't get in you?
When the Holy Spirit came down on Jesus like a dove,
Didn't God say, "This is my Son, my beloved!"

It takes Power from on High to walk down here,
To do battle with the enemy and have no fear,
To speak of what is written and to use the Name,
Of Jesus Christ the Savior you have claimed.

John the Baptist spoke from his own mouth,
That there was one to come that would bring about.
Not the water baptism of repenting from sin,
But Baptism with the Holy Ghost, and fire only from Him.

**-47-**

You're not done when you receive the Savior,
Go just one step further, do yourself a favor,
Ask the Lord for what He has promised,
Don't be caught being a doubting Thomas!

Don't just stop halfway through,
There is so much more the Lord has for you!

But it's not automatic you have to ask to receive,
You have to have faith and in Him believe,
That he will place His Holy Spirit in you,
A new creature to be born, with work to do.

He wants you to have Power from on High,
He wants to give you a new tongue and this is why,
That new tongue edifies only you,
It's a part of being reborn, becoming brand new.

Praying in the Spirit He commands every day,
It builds your faith, it's just the Lord's way.
I didn't make this up, it's all in the book,
Don't y'all go giving me that funny look.

The Holy Spirit wants to use your voice,
So give Him His way, come on, make that choice.
The Lord wants you to practice decreasing yourself,
As the Spirit increases and you partake of his wealth,

The Lord takes the foolish things of men to confound the wise,
Do not try to make sense of it or justify,
'Cause your intellect will get in the way,
And you can't receive what the Lord has for you today.

Only the sincere in heart that wants to receive,
With a childlike nature and a spirit that dares to believe,
That God will do His thing, and it will be alright,
He never needed to ask our advice.

So when the Holy Spirit wants those gifts to come out,
You'll get out the way and won't have a doubt.
That the Holy Spirit is ready to work through you,
To edify the Body or cast out -- you know who.

So go to the upper room, don't tarry dear,
Many have gone before, so have no fear,
I tell you these things so that you will be blessed,
And I won't be like John, crying in the wilderness.

**-49-**

Dr. Lydia A. Woods

# *The Time is Short!*

*Mark 13:20; Acts 1:7; I Thessalonians 5:1-2; II Peter 3 (KJV)*

The time must be shortened, so the scripture say,
For even the elect could be deceived in that day,

That latter day when the spirit of antichrist is full,
And sinners and saints have forgotten the golden rule.

To love one another, as He has loved us,
To give Him our hearts and in Him only trust.

The way is not straight and only He can be our guide,
Put your reasoning and thinking to the side,

For you cannot walk the straightway with the sight in your eyes,
Ask for understanding and wisdom; let it be your guide,

And that wisdom is found, in His Holy Spirit, you know,
Jesus left Him here to help show us the way to go.

He will lead you home, through this world of sin,
Without the Holy Spirit's help, you can never win,

That race that is given, only to them that endure,
With His guidance don't worry, your victory is sure.

Hurry my brothers and sisters, you I implore,
Come quickly through that tiny open Door,

Choose the Lord this day, while He may be found,
Stop wasting precious time just fooling around.

The time is short, the signs tell us day by day,
Listen, I beg you, to what I have to say,
Is my job truly hopeless, will "not anyone hear?
The Word said, In the latter days
They won't bear sound teaching," I fear!

Dr. Lydia A. Woods

# *Was He Saved? Did He Know the Lord?*

*John 13:34-35; I John 4:21 (KJV)*

When my father died,
My Christian friends asked me,
"Was he saved?
Did he know the Lord?"

I replied,

"I never heard him say he was a Christian,
I never heard him pray out loud,
He never went to church on Sunday,
While serving Jesus all the while.

He lived what Jesus commanded,
Never an unkind word that he spoke,
Loving his brother and sister in all his ways,
So humble in spirit did his manner denote.

He was a humble servant to many,
He was blessed all of his days,
I just marvel at the fruit he produced,
As he modeled Christ in his everyday ways.

I saw him pour out his life for others,
He never turned a man from his door,
He was filled with a knowing wisdom,
He had a heart and mind to explore.

And in that wisdom he never spoke of his faith,
Although he lived it in all of his ways,
There was never a doubt in my mind,
That he knew the Lord or was saved."

**-53-**

What is the greatest commandment,
That in doing you cover all the rest?
Love the Lord thy God with all thy
Heart, mind, soul and strength,
Love your brother as yourself and no less.

The heart of a man we will never know,
For that is given to the Lord,
But scripture tells us to try every spirit,
Using the Word like a two-edged sword.

The Bible reports that Jesus will say to many,
In the last days, I never knew you,
You never lived as I commanded,
You never did what I asked you to!

Look at the life of a man or woman,
Look at the fruit upon the tree,
Check for signs of full growth and ripeness,
It tells the truth of that person, you see.

Another person's Salvation,
Is between them and our Father above,
Let the Spirit bear witness and the Angels record,
"Was he saved? – Did He Know the Lord?"

# Scriptural
# References

# Adult vs Child

*Matthew 18:3; Proverbs 22:6; Luke 18:16 (KJV)*

**Matthew 18:3 (KJV)**
3 And said, Verily I say unto you, Except ye be converted, and become as little children, ye shall not enter into the kingdom of heaven.

**Proverbs 22:6 (KJV)**
6 Train up a child in the way he should go: and when he is old, he will not depart from it.

**Luke 18:16 (KJV)**
16 But Jesus called them unto him, and said, Suffer little children to come unto me, and forbid them not: for of such is the kingdom of God.

# *But For Your Praying Saints*

*Ephesians 6:18; I Thessalonians 5:17; James 5:16 (KJV)*

## Ephesians 6:18 (KJV)
[18] Praying always with all prayer and supplication in the Spirit, and watching thereunto with all perseverance and supplication for all saints;

## I Thessalonians 5:17 (KJV)
[17] Pray without ceasing.

## James 5:16 (KJV)
[16] Confess your faults one to another, and pray one for another, that ye may be healed. The effectual fervent prayer of a righteous man availeth much.

Dr. Lydia A. Woods

# Created in My Father's Image

*Philippians 2:6; Galatians 4:6 (KJV)*

**Philippians 2:6 (KJV)**
6 Who, being in the form of God, thought it not robbery to be equal with God:

**Galatians 4:6 (KJV)**
6 And because ye are sons, God hath sent forth the Spirit of his Son into your hearts, crying, Abba, Father.

# Don't Envy Those

*Malachi 3:13-18 (KJV)*

**Malachi 3:13-18 (KJV)**

[13] Your words have been stout against me, saith the LORD. Yet ye say, What have we spoken so much against thee?

[14] Ye have said, It is vain to serve God: and what profit is it that we have kept his ordinance, and that we have walked mournfully before the LORD of hosts?

[15] And now we call the proud happy; yea, they that work wickedness are set up; yea, they that tempt God are even delivered.

[16] Then they that feared the LORD spake often one to another: and the LORD hearkened, and heard it, and a book of remembrance was written before him for them that feared the LORD, and that thought upon his name.

[17] And they shall be mine, saith the LORD of hosts, in that day when I make up my jewels; and I will spare them, as a man spareth his own son that serveth him.

[18] Then shall ye return, and discern between the righteous and the wicked, between him that serveth God and him that serveth him not.

# *The Family Business*

*I Corinthians 3:7-9 (KJV)*

## I Corinthians 3:7-9 (KJV)
[7] So then neither is he that planteth any thing, neither he that watereth; but God that giveth the increase.
[8] Now he that planteth and he that watereth are one: and every man shall receive his own reward according to his own labour.
[9] For we are labourers together with God: ye are God's husbandry, ye are God's building.

# *Fear vs Faith*

*I John 4:18; Romans 8:15; Luke 12:32; Psalm 118:6 (KJV)*

## I John 4:18 (KJV)
[18] There is no fear in love; but perfect love casteth out fear: because fear hath torment. He that feareth is not made perfect in love.

## Romans 8:15 (KJV)
[15] For ye have not received the spirit of bondage again to fear; but ye have received the Spirit of adoption, whereby we cry, Abba, Father.

## Luke 12:32 (KJV)
[32] Fear not, little flock; for it is your Father's good pleasure to give you the kingdom.

## Psalm 118:6 (KJV)
[6] The LORD is on my side; I will not fear: what can man do unto me?

Dr. Lydia A. Woods

# *Go the Distance*

*Revelation 2:1-29, 3:1-22 (KJV)*

**Revelation 2:1-29 (KJV)**

¹ Unto the angel of the church of Ephesus write; These things saith he that holdeth the seven stars in his right hand, who walketh in the midst of the seven golden candlesticks;
² I know thy works, and thy labour, and thy patience, and how thou canst not bear them which are evil: and thou hast tried them which say they are apostles, and are not, and hast found them liars:
³ And hast borne, and hast patience, and for my name's sake hast laboured, and hast not fainted.
⁴ Nevertheless I have somewhat against thee, because thou hast left thy first love.
⁵ Remember therefore from whence thou art fallen, and repent, and do the first works; or else I will come unto thee quickly, and will remove thy candlestick out of his place, except thou repent.
⁶ But this thou hast, that thou hatest the deeds of the Nicolaitanes, which I also hate.
⁷ He that hath an ear, let him hear what the Spirit saith unto the churches; To him that overcometh will I give to eat of the tree of life, which is in the midst of the paradise of God.
⁸ And unto the angel of the church in Smyrna write; These things saith the first and the last, which was dead, and is alive;
⁹ I know thy works, and tribulation, and poverty, (but thou art rich) and I know the blasphemy of them which say they are Jews, and are not, but are the synagogue of Satan.
¹⁰ Fear none of those things which thou shalt suffer: behold, the devil shall cast some of you into prison, that ye may be tried; and ye shall have tribulation ten days: be thou faithful unto death, and I will give thee a crown of life.

-63-

<sup>11</sup> He that hath an ear, let him hear what the Spirit saith unto the churches; He that overcometh shall not be hurt of the second death.
<sup>12</sup> And to the angel of the church in Pergamos write; These things saith he which hath the sharp sword with two edges;
<sup>13</sup> I know thy works, and where thou dwellest, even where Satan's seat is: and thou holdest fast my name, and hast not denied my faith, even in those days wherein Antipas was my faithful martyr, who was slain among you, where Satan dwelleth.
<sup>14</sup> But I have a few things against thee, because thou hast there them that hold the doctrine of Balaam, who taught Balac to cast a stumblingblock before the children of Israel, to eat things sacrificed unto idols, and to commit fornication.
<sup>15</sup> So hast thou also them that hold the doctrine of the Nicolaitanes, which thing I hate.
<sup>16</sup> Repent; or else I will come unto thee quickly, and will fight against them with the sword of my mouth.
<sup>17</sup> He that hath an ear, let him hear what the Spirit saith unto the churches; To him that overcometh will I give to eat of the hidden manna, and will give him a white stone, and in the stone a new name written, which no man knoweth saving he that receiveth it.
<sup>18</sup> And unto the angel of the church in Thyatira write; These things saith the Son of God, who hath his eyes like unto a flame of fire, and his feet are like fine brass;
<sup>19</sup> I know thy works, and charity, and service, and faith, and thy patience, and thy works; and the last to be more than the first.
<sup>20</sup> Notwithstanding I have a few things against thee, because thou sufferest that woman Jezebel, which calleth herself a prophetess, to teach and to seduce my servants to commit fornication, and to eat things sacrificed unto idols.

**-64-**

21 And I gave her space to repent of her fornication; and she repented not.

22 Behold, I will cast her into a bed, and them that commit adultery with her into great tribulation, except they repent of their deeds.

23 And I will kill her children with death; and all the churches shall know that I am he which searcheth the reins and hearts: and I will give unto every one of you according to your works.

24 But unto you I say, and unto the rest in Thyatira, as many as have not this doctrine, and which have not known the depths of Satan, as they speak; I will put upon you none other burden.

25 But that which ye have already hold fast till I come.

26 And he that overcometh, and keepeth my works unto the end, to him will I give power over the nations:

27 And he shall rule them with a rod of iron; as the vessels of a potter shall they be broken to shivers: even as I received of my Father.

28 And I will give him the morning star.

29 He that hath an ear, let him hear what the Spirit saith unto the churches.

### Revelation 3:1-22 (KJV)

1 And unto the angel of the church in Sardis write; These things saith he that hath the seven Spirits of God, and the seven stars; I know thy works, that thou hast a name that thou livest, and art dead.

2 Be watchful, and strengthen the things which remain, that are ready to die: for I have not found thy works perfect before God.

³ Remember therefore how thou hast received and heard, and hold fast, and repent. If therefore thou shalt not watch, I will come on thee as a thief, and thou shalt not know what hour I will come upon thee.

⁴ Thou hast a few names even in Sardis which have not defiled their garments; and they shall walk with me in white: for they are worthy.

⁵ He that overcometh, the same shall be clothed in white raiment; and I will not blot out his name out of the book of life, but I will confess his name before my Father, and before his angels.

⁶ He that hath an ear, let him hear what the Spirit saith unto the churches.

⁷ And to the angel of the church in Philadelphia write; These things saith he that is holy, he that is true, he that hath the key of David, he that openeth, and no man shutteth; and shutteth, and no man openeth;

⁸ I know thy works: behold, I have set before thee an open door, and no man can shut it: for thou hast a little strength, and hast kept my word, and hast not denied my name.

⁹ Behold, I will make them of the synagogue of Satan, which say they are Jews, and are not, but do lie; behold, I will make them to come and worship before thy feet, and to know that I have loved thee.

¹⁰ Because thou hast kept the word of my patience, I also will keep thee from the hour of temptation, which shall come upon all the world, to try them that dwell upon the earth.

¹¹ Behold, I come quickly: hold that fast which thou hast, that no man take thy crown.

<sup>12</sup> Him that overcometh will I make a pillar in the temple of my God, and he shall go no more out: and I will write upon him the name of my God, and the name of the city of my God, which is new Jerusalem, which cometh down out of heaven from my God: and I will write upon him my new name.

<sup>13</sup> He that hath an ear, let him hear what the Spirit saith unto the churches.

<sup>14</sup> And unto the angel of the church of the Laodiceans write; These things saith the Amen, the faithful and true witness, the beginning of the creation of God;

<sup>15</sup> I know thy works, that thou art neither cold nor hot: I would thou wert cold or hot.

<sup>16</sup> So then because thou art lukewarm, and neither cold nor hot, I will spue thee out of my mouth.

<sup>17</sup> Because thou sayest, I am rich, and increased with goods, and have need of nothing; and knowest not that thou art wretched, and miserable, and poor, and blind, and naked:

<sup>18</sup> I counsel thee to buy of me gold tried in the fire, that thou mayest be rich; and white raiment, that thou mayest be clothed, and that the shame of thy nakedness do not appear; and anoint thine eyes with eyesalve, that thou mayest see.

<sup>19</sup> As many as I love, I rebuke and chasten: be zealous therefore, and repent.

<sup>20</sup> Behold, I stand at the door, and knock: if any man hear my voice, and open the door, I will come in to him, and will sup with him, and he with me.

21 To him that overcometh will I grant to sit with me in my throne, even as I also overcame, and am set down with my Father in his throne.
22 He that hath an ear, let him hear what the Spirit saith unto the churches.

Dr. Lydia A. Woods

# *God Will Provide*

*Genesis 22:1-19 (KJV)*

## Genesis 22:1-19 (KJV)

<sup>1</sup> And it came to pass after these things, that God did tempt Abraham, and said unto him, Abraham: and he said, Behold, here I am.

<sup>2</sup> And he said, Take now thy son, thine only son Isaac, whom thou lovest, and get thee into the land of Moriah; and offer him there for a burnt offering upon one of the mountains which I will tell thee of.

<sup>3</sup> And Abraham rose up early in the morning, and saddled his ass, and took two of his young men with him, and Isaac his son, and clave the wood for the burnt offering, and rose up, and went unto the place of which God had told him.

<sup>4</sup> Then on the third day Abraham lifted up his eyes, and saw the place afar off.

<sup>5</sup> And Abraham said unto his young men, Abide ye here with the ass; and I and the lad will go yonder and worship, and come again to you.

<sup>6</sup> And Abraham took the wood of the burnt offering, and laid it upon Isaac his son; and he took the fire in his hand, and a knife; and they went both of them together.

<sup>7</sup> And Isaac spake unto Abraham his father, and said, My father: and he said, Here am I, my son. And he said, Behold the fire and the wood: but where is the lamb for a burnt offering?

<sup>8</sup> And Abraham said, My son, God will provide himself a lamb for a burnt offering: so they went both of them together.

<sup>9</sup> And they came to the place which God had told him of; and Abraham built an altar there, and laid the wood in order, and bound Isaac his son, and laid him on the altar upon the wood.

<sup>10</sup> And Abraham stretched forth his hand, and took the knife to slay his son.

-69-

<sup>11</sup> And the angel of the LORD called unto him out of heaven, and said, Abraham, Abraham: and he said, Here am I.

<sup>12</sup> And he said, Lay not thine hand upon the lad, neither do thou any thing unto him: for now I know that thou fearest God, seeing thou hast not withheld thy son, thine only son from me.

<sup>13</sup> And Abraham lifted up his eyes, and looked, and behold behind him a ram caught in a thicket by his horns: and Abraham went and took the ram, and offered him up for a burnt offering in the stead of his son.

<sup>14</sup> And Abraham called the name of that place Jehovahjireh: as it is said to this day, In the mount of the LORD it shall be seen.

<sup>15</sup> And the angel of the LORD called unto Abraham out of heaven the second time,

<sup>16</sup> And said, By myself have I sworn, saith the LORD, for because thou hast done this thing, and hast not withheld thy son, thine only son:

<sup>17</sup> That in blessing I will bless thee, and in multiplying I will multiply thy seed as the stars of the heaven, and as the sand which is upon the sea shore; and thy seed shall possess the gate of his enemies;

<sup>18</sup> And in thy seed shall all the nations of the earth be blessed; because thou hast obeyed my voice.

<sup>19</sup> So Abraham returned unto his young men, and they rose up and went together to Beersheba; and Abraham dwelt at Beersheba.

# Group Three

*Matthew 8:12, 13:37-43; Luke 13:24-30 (KJV)*

## Matthew 8:12 (KJV)
12 But the children of the kingdom shall be cast out into outer darkness: there shall be weeping and gnashing of teeth.

## Matthew 13:37-43 (KJV)
37 He answered and said unto them, He that soweth the good seed is the Son of man;
38 The field is the world; the good seed are the children of the kingdom; but the tares are the children of the wicked one;
39 The enemy that sowed them is the devil; the harvest is the end of the world; and the reapers are the angels.
40 As therefore the tares are gathered and burned in the fire; so shall it be in the end of this world.
41 The Son of man shall send forth his angels, and they shall gather out of his kingdom all things that offend, and them which do iniquity;
42 And shall cast them into a furnace of fire: there shall be wailing and gnashing of teeth.
43 Then shall the righteous shine forth as the sun in the kingdom of their Father. Who hath ears to hear, let him hear.

## Luke 13:24-30 (KJV)
24 Strive to enter in at the strait gate: for many, I say unto you, will seek to enter in, and shall not be able.
25 When once the master of the house is risen up, and hath shut to the door, and ye begin to stand without, and to knock at the door, saying, Lord, Lord, open unto us; and he shall answer and say unto you, I know you not whence ye are:
26 Then shall ye begin to say, We have eaten and drunk in thy presence, and thou hast taught in our streets.

[27] But he shall say, I tell you, I know you not whence ye are; depart from me, all ye workers of iniquity.

[28] There shall be weeping and gnashing of teeth, when ye shall see Abraham, and Isaac, and Jacob, and all the prophets, in the kingdom of God, and you yourselves thrust out.

[29] And they shall come from the east, and from the west, and from the north, and from the south, and shall sit down in the kingdom of God.

[30] And, behold, there are last which shall be first, and there are first which shall be last.

# *Hedge of Protection*

*Psalm 91:1-16; I Peter 3:4-6 (KJV)*

## Psalm 91:1-16 (KJV)

1 He that dwelleth in the secret place of the most High shall abide under the shadow of the Almighty.

2 I will say of the LORD, He is my refuge and my fortress: my God; in him will I trust.

3 Surely he shall deliver thee from the snare of the fowler, and from the noisome pestilence.

4 He shall cover thee with his feathers, and under his wings shalt thou trust: his truth shall be thy shield and buckler.

5 Thou shalt not be afraid for the terror by night; nor for the arrow that flieth by day;

6 Nor for the pestilence that walketh in darkness; nor for the destruction that wasteth at noonday.

7 A thousand shall fall at thy side, and ten thousand at thy right hand; but it shall not come nigh thee.

8 Only with thine eyes shalt thou behold and see the reward of the wicked.

9 Because thou hast made the LORD, which is my refuge, even the most High, thy habitation;

10 There shall no evil befall thee, neither shall any plague come nigh thy dwelling.

11 For he shall give his angels charge over thee, to keep thee in all thy ways.

12 They shall bear thee up in their hands, lest thou dash thy foot against a stone.

13 Thou shalt tread upon the lion and adder: the young lion and the dragon shalt thou trample under feet.

14 Because he hath set his love upon me, therefore will I deliver him: I will set him on high, because he hath known my name.

**-73-**

[15] He shall call upon me, and I will answer him: I will be with him in trouble; I will deliver him, and honour him.
[16] With long life will I satisfy him, and shew him my salvation.

**I Peter 3:4-6 (KJV)**
[4] But let it be the hidden man of the heart, in that which is not corruptible, even the ornament of a meek and quiet spirit, which is in the sight of God of great price.
[5] For after this manner in the old time the holy women also, who trusted in God, adorned themselves, being in subjection unto their own husbands:
[6] Even as Sara obeyed Abraham, calling him lord: whose daughters ye are, as long as ye do well, and are not afraid with any amazement.

Dr. Lydia A. Woods

# *How Many Times*

*Philippians 4:19 (KJV)*

**Philippians 4:19 (KJV)**
[19] But my God shall supply all your need according to his riches in glory by Christ Jesus.

*A Collection of Christian Poems*                          *How Many Times*

# *How Will I Know Him?*

*Genesis 24:1-67 (KJV)*

## Genesis 24:1-67 (KJV)

[1] And Abraham was old, and well stricken in age: and the LORD had blessed Abraham in all things.

[2] And Abraham said unto his eldest servant of his house, that ruled over all that he had, Put, I pray thee, thy hand under my thigh:

[3] And I will make thee swear by the LORD, the God of heaven, and the God of the earth, that thou shalt not take a wife unto my son of the daughters of the Canaanites, among whom I dwell:

[4] But thou shalt go unto my country, and to my kindred, and take a wife unto my son Isaac.

[5] And the servant said unto him, Peradventure the woman will not be willing to follow me unto this land: must I needs bring thy son again unto the land from whence thou camest?

[6] And Abraham said unto him, Beware thou that thou bring not my son thither again.

[7] The LORD God of heaven, which took me from my father's house, and from the land of my kindred, and which spake unto me, and that sware unto me, saying, Unto thy seed will I give this land; he shall send his angel before thee, and thou shalt take a wife unto my son from thence.

[8] And if the woman will not be willing to follow thee, then thou shalt be clear from this my oath: only bring not my son thither again.

[9] And the servant put his hand under the thigh of Abraham his master, and sware to him concerning that matter.

[10] And the servant took ten camels of the camels of his master, and departed; for all the goods of his master were in his hand: and he arose, and went to Mesopotamia, unto the city of Nahor.

<sup>11</sup> And he made his camels to kneel down without the city by a well of water at the time of the evening, even the time that women go out to draw water.

<sup>12</sup> And he said O LORD God of my master Abraham, I pray thee, send me good speed this day, and shew kindness unto my master Abraham.

<sup>13</sup> Behold, I stand here by the well of water; and the daughters of the men of the city come out to draw water:

<sup>14</sup> And let it come to pass, that the damsel to whom I shall say, Let down thy pitcher, I pray thee, that I may drink; and she shall say, Drink, and I will give thy camels drink also: let the same be she that thou hast appointed for thy servant Isaac; and thereby shall I know that thou hast shewed kindness unto my master.

<sup>15</sup> And it came to pass, before he had done speaking, that, behold, Rebekah came out, who was born to Bethuel, son of Milcah, the wife of Nahor, Abraham's brother, with her pitcher upon her shoulder.

<sup>16</sup> And the damsel was very fair to look upon, a virgin, neither had any man known her: and she went down to the well, and filled her pitcher, and came up.

<sup>17</sup> And the servant ran to meet her, and said, Let me, I pray thee, drink a little water of thy pitcher.

<sup>18</sup> And she said, Drink, my lord: and she hasted, and let down her pitcher upon her hand, and gave him drink.

<sup>19</sup> And when she had done giving him drink, she said, I will draw water for thy camels also, until they have done drinking.

<sup>20</sup> And she hasted, and emptied her pitcher into the trough, and ran again unto the well to draw water, and drew for all his camels.

<sup>21</sup> And the man wondering at her held his peace, to wit whether the LORD had made his journey prosperous or not.

<sup>22</sup> And it came to pass, as the camels had done drinking, that the man took a golden earring of half a shekel weight, and two bracelets for her hands of ten shekels weight of gold;

<sup>23</sup> And said, Whose daughter art thou? tell me, I pray thee: is there room in thy father's house for us to lodge in?

<sup>24</sup> And she said unto him, I am the daughter of Bethuel the son of Milcah, which she bare unto Nahor.

<sup>25</sup> She said moreover unto him, We have both straw and provender enough, and room to lodge in.

<sup>26</sup> And the man bowed down his head, and worshipped the LORD.

<sup>27</sup> And he said, Blessed be the LORD God of my master Abraham, who hath not left destitute my master of his mercy and his truth: I being in the way, the LORD led me to the house of my master's brethren.

<sup>28</sup> And the damsel ran, and told them of her mother's house these things.

<sup>29</sup> And Rebekah had a brother, and his name was Laban: and Laban ran out unto the man, unto the well.

<sup>30</sup> And it came to pass, when he saw the earring and bracelets upon his sister's hands, and when he heard the words of Rebekah his sister, saying, Thus spake the man unto me; that he came unto the man; and, behold, he stood by the camels at the well.

<sup>31</sup> And he said, Come in, thou blessed of the LORD; wherefore standest thou without? for I have prepared the house, and room for the camels.

<sup>32</sup> And the man came into the house: and he ungirded his camels, and gave straw and provender for the camels, and water to wash his feet, and the men's feet that were with him.

<sup>33</sup> And there was set meat before him to eat: but he said, I will not eat, until I have told mine errand. And he said, Speak on.

<sup>34</sup> And he said, I am Abraham's servant.

<sup>35</sup> And the LORD hath blessed my master greatly; and he is become great: and he hath given him flocks, and herds, and silver, and gold, and menservants, and maidservants, and camels, and asses.

<sup>36</sup> And Sarah my master's wife bare a son to my master when she was old: and unto him hath he given all that he hath.

<sup>37</sup> And my master made me swear, saying, Thou shalt not take a wife to my son of the daughters of the Canaanites, in whose land I dwell:

<sup>38</sup> But thou shalt go unto my father's house, and to my kindred, and take a wife unto my son.

<sup>39</sup> And I said unto my master, Peradventure the woman will not follow me.

<sup>40</sup> And he said unto me, The LORD, before whom I walk, will send his angel with thee, and prosper thy way; and thou shalt take a wife for my son of my kindred, and of my father's house:

<sup>41</sup> Then shalt thou be clear from this my oath, when thou comest to my kindred; and if they give not thee one, thou shalt be clear from my oath.

<sup>42</sup> And I came this day unto the well, and said, O LORD God of my master Abraham, if now thou do prosper my way which I go:

<sup>43</sup> Behold, I stand by the well of water; and it shall come to pass, that when the virgin cometh forth to draw water, and I say to her, Give me, I pray thee, a little water of thy pitcher to drink;

<sup>44</sup> And she say to me, Both drink thou, and I will also draw for thy camels: let the same be the woman whom the LORD hath appointed out for my master's son.

<sup>45</sup> And before I had done speaking in mine heart, behold, Rebekah came forth with her pitcher on her shoulder; and she went down unto the well, and drew water: and I said unto her, Let me drink, I pray thee.

<sup>46</sup> And she made haste, and let down her pitcher from her shoulder, and said, Drink, and I will give thy camels drink also: so I drank, and she made the camels drink also.

<sup>47</sup> And I asked her, and said, Whose daughter art thou? And she said, the daughter of Bethuel, Nahor's son, whom Milcah bare unto him: and I put the earring upon her face, and the bracelets upon her hands.

<sup>48</sup> And I bowed down my head, and worshipped the LORD, and blessed the LORD God of my master Abraham, which had led me in the right way to take my master's brother's daughter unto his son.

<sup>49</sup> And now if ye will deal kindly and truly with my master, tell me: and if not, tell me; that I may turn to the right hand, or to the left.

<sup>50</sup> Then Laban and Bethuel answered and said, The thing proceedeth from the LORD: we cannot speak unto thee bad or good.

<sup>51</sup> Behold, Rebekah is before thee, take her, and go, and let her be thy master's son's wife, as the LORD hath spoken.

<sup>52</sup> And it came to pass, that, when Abraham's servant heard their words, he worshipped the LORD, bowing himself to the earth.

<sup>53</sup> And the servant brought forth jewels of silver, and jewels of gold, and raiment, and gave them to Rebekah: he gave also to her brother and to her mother precious things.

**-80-**

<sup>54</sup> And they did eat and drink, he and the men that were with him, and tarried all night; and they rose up in the morning, and he said, Send me away unto my master.
<sup>55</sup> And her brother and her mother said, Let the damsel abide with us a few days, at the least ten; after that she shall go.
<sup>56</sup> And he said unto them, Hinder me not, seeing the LORD hath prospered my way; send me away that I may go to my master.
<sup>57</sup> And they said, We will call the damsel, and enquire at her mouth.
<sup>58</sup> And they called Rebekah, and said unto her, Wilt thou go with this man? And she said, I will go.
<sup>59</sup> And they sent away Rebekah their sister, and her nurse, and Abraham's servant, and his men.
<sup>60</sup> And they blessed Rebekah, and said unto her, Thou art our sister, be thou the mother of thousands of millions, and let thy seed possess the gate of those which hate them.
<sup>61</sup> And Rebekah arose, and her damsels, and they rode upon the camels, and followed the man: and the servant took Rebekah, and went his way.
<sup>62</sup> And Isaac came from the way of the well Lahairoi; for he dwelt in the south country.
<sup>63</sup> And Isaac went out to meditate in the field at the eventide: and he lifted up his eyes, and saw, and, behold, the camels were coming.
<sup>64</sup> And Rebekah lifted up her eyes, and when she saw Isaac, she lighted off the camel.
<sup>65</sup> For she had said unto the servant, What man is this that walketh in the field to meet us? And the servant had said, It is my master: therefore she took a vail, and covered herself.
<sup>66</sup> And the servant told Isaac all things that he had done.

67 And Isaac brought her into his mother Sarah's tent, and took Rebekah, and she became his wife; and he loved her: and Isaac was comforted after his mother's death.

Dr. Lydia A. Woods

# I Need the Eyes of Jesus

*Luke 4:18; Psalm 119:105; I Corinthians 3:16 (KJV)*

## Luke 4:18 (KJV)
18 The Spirit of the Lord is upon me, because he hath anointed me to preach the gospel to the poor; he hath sent me to heal the brokenhearted, to preach deliverance to the captives, and recovering of sight to the blind, to set at liberty them that are bruised,

## Psalm 119:105 (KJV)
105 Thy word is a lamp unto my feet, and a light unto my path.

## I Corinthians 3:16 (KJV)
16 Know ye not that ye are the temple of God, and that the Spirit of God dwelleth in you?

*A Collection of Christian Poems*        *I Need the Eyes of Jesus*

# *If You Want to Make God Laugh!*

*Proverbs 19:21; Matthew 5:36; Isaiah 46:9-11 (KJV)*

## Proverbs 19:21 (KJV)
21 There are many devices in a man's heart; nevertheless the counsel of the LORD, that shall stand.

## Matthew 5:36 (KJV)
36 Neither shalt thou swear by thy head, because thou canst not make one hair white or black.

## Isaiah 46:9-11 (KJV)
9 Remember the former things of old: for I am God, and there is none else; I am God, and there is none like me,
10 Declaring the end from the beginning, and from ancient times the things that are not yet done, saying, My counsel shall stand, and I will do all my pleasure:
11 Calling a ravenous bird from the east, the man that executeth my counsel from a far country: yea, I have spoken it, I will also bring it to pass; I have purposed it, I will also do it.

# In a Split Second

*James 1:8; II Corinthians 10:5 (KJV)*

## James 1:8 (KJV)
[8] A double minded man is unstable in all his ways.

## II Corinthians 10:5 (KJV)
[5] Casting down imaginations, and every high thing that exalteth itself against the knowledge of God, and bringing into captivity every thought to the obedience of Christ;

**-85-**

# The Inside of the Cup

*Matthew 23:25; Luke 11:39 (KJV)*

## Matthew 23:25 (KJV)

25 Woe unto you, scribes and Pharisees, hypocrites! for ye make clean the outside of the cup and of the platter, but within they are full of extortion and excess.

## Luke 11:39 (KJV)

39 And the Lord said unto him, Now do ye Pharisees make clean the outside of the cup and the platter; but your inward part is full of ravening and wickedness.

Dr. Lydia A. Woods

# It's Not About Money

*Luke 12:22-34; Matthew 6:25-34 (KJV)*

## Luke 12:22-34 (KJV)

22 And he said unto his disciples, Therefore I say unto you, Take no thought for your life, what ye shall eat; neither for the body, what ye shall put on.

23 The life is more than meat, and the body is more than raiment.

24 Consider the ravens: for they neither sow nor reap; which neither have storehouse nor barn; and God feedeth them: how much more are ye better than the fowls?

25 And which of you with taking thought can add to his stature one cubit?

26 If ye then be not able to do that thing which is least, why take ye thought for the rest?

27 Consider the lilies how they grow: they toil not, they spin not; and yet I say unto you, that Solomon in all his glory was not arrayed like one of these.

28 If then God so clothe the grass, which is to day in the field, and to morrow is cast into the oven; how much more will he clothe you, O ye of little faith?

29 And seek not ye what ye shall eat, or what ye shall drink, neither be ye of doubtful mind.

30 For all these things do the nations of the world seek after: and your Father knoweth that ye have need of these things.

31 But rather seek ye the kingdom of God; and all these things shall be added unto you.

32 Fear not, little flock; for it is your Father's good pleasure to give you the kingdom.

33 Sell that ye have, and give alms; provide yourselves bags which wax not old, a treasure in the heavens that faileth not, where no thief approacheth, neither moth corrupteth.

-87-

34 For where your treasure is, there will your heart be also.

## Matthew 6:25-34 (KJV)

25 Therefore I say unto you, Take no thought for your life, what ye shall eat, or what ye shall drink; nor yet for your body, what ye shall put on. Is not the life more than meat, and the body than raiment?

26 Behold the fowls of the air: for they sow not, neither do they reap, nor gather into barns; yet your heavenly Father feedeth them. Are ye not much better than they?

27 Which of you by taking thought can add one cubit unto his stature?

28 And why take ye thought for raiment? Consider the lilies of the field, how they grow; they toil not, neither do they spin:

29 And yet I say unto you, That even Solomon in all his glory was not arrayed like one of these.

30 Wherefore, if God so clothe the grass of the field, which to day is, and to morrow is cast into the oven, shall he not much more clothe you, O ye of little faith?

31 Therefore take no thought, saying, What shall we eat? or, What shall we drink? or, Wherewithal shall we be clothed?

32 (For after all these things do the Gentiles seek:) for your heavenly Father knoweth that ye have need of all these things.

33 But seek ye first the kingdom of God, and his righteousness; and all these things shall be added unto you.

34 Take therefore no thought for the morrow: for the morrow shall take thought for the things of itself. Sufficient unto the day is the evil thereof.

Dr. Lydia A. Woods

# Oh! To be Like the Master

*John 8:12, 28-29, 31 (KJV)*

**John 8:12 (KJV)**
[12] Then spake Jesus again unto them, saying, I am the light of the world: he that followeth me shall not walk in darkness, but shall have the light of life.

**John 8:28-29 (KJV)**
[28] Then said Jesus unto them, When ye have lifted up the Son of man, then shall ye know that I am he, and that I do nothing of myself; but as my Father hath taught me, I speak these things.
[29] And he that sent me is with me: the Father hath not left me alone; for I do always those things that please him.

**John 8:31 (KJV)**
[31] Then said Jesus to those Jews which believed on him, If ye continue in my word, then are ye my disciples indeed;

## Somethin' Told Me

*John 12:26; Ephesians 4:30; Luke 2:26 (KJV)*

**John 12:26 (KJV)**
[26] If any man serve me, let him follow me; and where I am, there shall also my servant be: if any man serve me, him will my Father honour.

**Ephesians 4:30 (KJV)**
[30] And grieve not the holy Spirit of God, whereby ye are sealed unto the day of redemption.

**Luke 2:26 (KJV)**
[26] And it was revealed unto him by the Holy Ghost, that he should not see death, before he had seen the Lord's Christ.

-90-

*Somethin' Told Me*        *A Collection of Christian Poems*

# Take a Visit to the Upper Room

*Acts 1:3-4, 8, 2:1-21 (KJV)*

## Acts 1:3-4 (KJV)

3 To whom also he shewed himself alive after his passion by many infallible proofs, being seen of them forty days, and speaking of the things pertaining to the kingdom of God:
4 And, being assembled together with them, commanded them that they should not depart from Jerusalem, but wait for the promise of the Father, which, saith he, ye have heard of me.

## Acts 1:8 (KJV)

8 But ye shall receive power, after that the Holy Ghost is come upon you: and ye shall be witnesses unto me both in Jerusalem, and in all Judaea, and in Samaria, and unto the uttermost part of the earth.

## Acts 2:1-21 (KJV)

1 And when the day of Pentecost was fully come, they were all with one accord in one place.
2 And suddenly there came a sound from heaven as of a rushing mighty wind, and it filled all the house where they were sitting.
3 And there appeared unto them cloven tongues like as of fire, and it sat upon each of them.
4 And they were all filled with the Holy Ghost, and began to speak with other tongues, as the Spirit gave them utterance.
5 And there were dwelling at Jerusalem Jews, devout men, out of every nation under heaven.
6 Now when this was noised abroad, the multitude came together, and were confounded, because that every man heard them speak in his own language.
7 And they were all amazed and marvelled, saying one to another, Behold, are not all these which speak Galilaeans?

[8] And how hear we every man in our own tongue, wherein we were born?

[9] Parthians, and Medes, and Elamites, and the dwellers in Mesopotamia, and in Judaea, and Cappadocia, in Pontus, and Asia,

[10] Phrygia, and Pamphylia, in Egypt, and in the parts of Libya about Cyrene, and strangers of Rome, Jews and proselytes,

[11] Cretes and Arabians, we do hear them speak in our tongues the wonderful works of God.

[12] And they were all amazed, and were in doubt, saying one to another, What meaneth this?

[13] Others mocking said, These men are full of new wine.

[14] But Peter, standing up with the eleven, lifted up his voice, and said unto them, Ye men of Judaea, and all ye that dwell at Jerusalem, be this known unto you, and hearken to my words:

[15] For these are not drunken, as ye suppose, seeing it is but the third hour of the day.

[16] But this is that which was spoken by the prophet Joel;

[17] And it shall come to pass in the last days, saith God, I will pour out of my Spirit upon all flesh: and your sons and your daughters shall prophesy, and your young men shall see visions, and your old men shall dream dreams:

[18] And on my servants and on my handmaidens I will pour out in those days of my Spirit; and they shall prophesy:

[19] And I will shew wonders in heaven above, and signs in the earth beneath; blood, and fire, and vapour of smoke:

[20] The sun shall be turned into darkness, and the moon into blood, before the great and notable day of the Lord come:

[21] And it shall come to pass, that whosoever shall call on the name of the Lord shall be saved.

# *The Time is Short!*

*Mark 13:20; Acts 1:7; I Thessalonians 5:1-2; II Peter 3  (KJV)*

## Mark 13:20 (KJV)
20 And except that the Lord had shortened those days, no flesh should be saved: but for the elect's sake, whom he hath chosen, he hath shortened the days.

## Acts 1:7 (KJV)
7 And he said unto them, It is not for you to know the times or the seasons, which the Father hath put in his own power.

## I Thessalonians 5:1-2 (KJV)
1 But of the times and the seasons, brethren, ye have no need that I write unto you.
2 For yourselves know perfectly that the day of the Lord so cometh as a thief in the night.

## II Peter 3  (KJV)
1 This second epistle, beloved, I now write unto you; in both which I stir up your pure minds by way of remembrance:
2 That ye may be mindful of the words which were spoken before by the holy prophets, and of the commandment of us the apostles of the Lord and Saviour:
3 Knowing this first, that there shall come in the last days scoffers, walking after their own lusts,
4 And saying, Where is the promise of his coming? for since the fathers fell asleep, all things continue as they were from the beginning of the creation.
5 For this they willingly are ignorant of, that by the word of God the heavens were of old, and the earth standing out of the water and in the water:

6 Whereby the world that then was, being overflowed with water, perished:

7 But the heavens and the earth, which are now, by the same word are kept in store, reserved unto fire against the day of judgment and perdition of ungodly men.

8 But, beloved, be not ignorant of this one thing, that one day is with the Lord as a thousand years, and a thousand years as one day.

9 The Lord is not slack concerning his promise, as some men count slackness; but is longsuffering to us-ward, not willing that any should perish, but that all should come to repentance.

10 But the day of the Lord will come as a thief in the night; in the which the heavens shall pass away with a great noise, and the elements shall melt with fervent heat, the earth also and the works that are therein shall be burned up.

11 Seeing then that all these things shall be dissolved, what manner of persons ought ye to be in all holy conversation and godliness,

12 Looking for and hasting unto the coming of the day of God, wherein the heavens being on fire shall be dissolved, and the elements shall melt with fervent heat?

13 Nevertheless we, according to his promise, look for new heavens and a new earth, wherein dwelleth righteousness.

14 Wherefore, beloved, seeing that ye look for such things, be diligent that ye may be found of him in peace, without spot, and blameless.

15 And account that the longsuffering of our Lord is salvation; even as our beloved brother Paul also according to the wisdom given unto him hath written unto you;

*The Time is Short!*                    *A Collection of Christian Poems*

<sup>16</sup> As also in all his epistles, speaking in them of these things; in which are some things hard to be understood, which they that are unlearned and unstable wrest, as they do also the other scriptures, unto their own destruction.

<sup>17</sup> Ye therefore, beloved, seeing ye know these things before, beware lest ye also, being led away with the error of the wicked, fall from your own stedfastness.

<sup>18</sup> But grow in grace, and in the knowledge of our Lord and Saviour Jesus Christ. To him be glory both now and for ever. Amen.

# Was He Saved? Did He Know the Lord?

*John 13:34-35; I John 4:21 (KJV)*

## John 13:34-35 (KJV)

34 A new commandment I give unto you, That ye love one another; as I have loved you, that ye also love one another.
35 By this shall all men know that ye are my disciples, if ye have love one to another.

## I John 4:21 (KJV)

21 And this commandment have we from him, That he who loveth God love his brother also.

-96-

*Was He Saved? Did He Know the Lord?*     *A Collection of Christian Poems*

# Scriptural
# Index

**Genesis**
22:1-19
God Will Provide, 17, 69
24:1-67
How Will I Know Him?, 26, 76
**Psalms**
91:1-16
Hedge of Protection, 21, 73
118:6
Fear vs Faith, 11, 62
119:105
I Need the Eyes of Jesus, 27,
83
**Proverbs**
19:21
If You Want to Make God
Laugh!, 29, 84
22:6
Adult vs Child, 1, 57
**Isaiah**
46:9-11
If You Want to Make God
Laugh!, 29, 84
**Malachi**
3:13-18
Don't Envy Those, 7, 60
**Matthew**
5:36
If You Want to Make God
Laugh!, 29, 84
6:25-34
It's Not About Money, 37, 88
8:12
Group Three, 19, 71
13:37-43
Group Three, 19, 71
18:3
Adult vs Child, 1, 57
23:25
The Inside of the Cup, 35, 86

**Mark**
13:20
The Time is Short!, 51, 93
**Luke**
2:26
Somethin' Told Me, 45, 90
4:18
I Need the Eyes of Jesus, 27,
83
11:39
The Inside of the Cup, 35, 86
12:22-34
It's Not About Money, 37, 87
12:32
Fear vs Faith, 11, 62
13:24-30
Group Three, 19, 71
18:16
Adult vs Child, 1, 57
**John**
8:12
Oh! To be Like the Master, 39,
89
8:28-29
Oh! To be Like the Master, 39,
89
8:31
Oh! To be Like the Master, 39,
89
12:26
Somethin' Told Me, 45, 90
13:34-35
Was He Saved? Did He Know
the Lord?, 53, 96
**Acts**
1:3-4
Take a Visit to the Upper
Room, 47, 91
1:7
The Time is Short!, 51, 93

1:8
Take a Visit to the Upper
Room, 47, 91
2:1-21
Take a Visit to the Upper
Room, 47, 91
**Romans**
8:15
Fear vs Faith, 11, 62
**I Corinthians**
3:7-9
The Family Business, 9, 61
3:16
I Need the Eyes of Jesus, 27,
83
**II Corinthians**
10:5
In a Split Second, 31, 85
**Galatians**
4:6
Created in My Father's Image,
5, 59
**Ephesians**
4:30
Somethin' Told Me, 45, 90
6:18
But For Your Praying Saints, 3,
58
**Philippians**
2:6
Created in My Father's Image,
5, 59

4:19
How Many Times, 23, 75
**I Thessalonians**
5:1-2
The Time is Short!, 51, 93
5:17
But For Your Praying Saints, 3,
58
**James**
1:8
In a Split Second, 31, 85
5:16
But For Your Praying Saints, 3,
58
**I Peter**
3:4-6
Hedge of Protection, 21, 74
**II Peter**
3
The Time is Short!, 51, 93
**I John**
4:18
Fear vs Faith, 11, 62
4:21
Was He Saved? Did He Know
the Lord?, 53, 96
**Revelations**
2:1-29
Go the Distance, 13, 63
3:1-22
Go the Distance, 13, 65

**-100-**

www.ingramcontent.com/pod-product-compliance
Lightning Source LLC
Chambersburg PA
CBHW061752020426
42331CB00006B/1448

*9 7 8 1 9 4 1 2 0 0 1 4 8 *